D1560858

FARMING COMES OF AGE

The Remarkable Photographs of J. C. Allen & Son

THE LAND

THE FAMILY

THE BOUNTY

FARMING COMES OF AGE

The Remarkable Photographs of J. C. Allen & Son

1912 to 1942

FARM PROGRESS COMPANIES, INC.

IN ASSOCIATION WITH

HARMONY HOUSE PUBLISHERS

This Book is Dedicated to J. C. Allen

Executive Editor: Thomas Budd
Photographic Editor: William H. Strode
Copy Editor: Claude L. Brock
Production Manager: Doug Bartholomew
Printed in Canada
First printing: 1995
ISBN 1-56469-024-5
Library of Congress 94-077068
Copyright © 1995 Farm Progress Companies, Inc.
Carol Stream, Illinois
In association with Harmony House Publishers
Louisville, Kentucky
Photographs Copyright © J. C. Allen & Son
West Lafayette, Indiana
All Rights Reserved

FOREWORD

American farm families are more than providers of food and fiber for the world. The lifestyle, standards and work ethics which have been established by those who till the soil are good examples for the world.

"Farming Comes Of Age" preserves forever images of people, the places, the animals, the machines and the times which have made American agriculture the greatest productive force on earth.

Vision and commitment were required on the part of select individuals to complete this valuable photographic history of America's agricultural Midwest. We salute the vision and dedication of the following people who were key to the development of this important book:

J. C. Allen; Founder of J. C. Allen & Son Rural Life Photo Service.
Chester Allen; Son of J. C. Allen who carried on the excellent photographic tradition of his father.
John Allen; Son of Chester Allen who has supported and participated in the work of his father during these modern times.
Thomas Budd; Vice President and Publisher of the Farm Progress Companies, a writer whose dedication to agriculture spurred the decision and resources necessary to publish this valuable addition to American farm history.

It is the hope of all that American agriculture will continue to be a source of sustenance for the world's population and a wellspring which gives birth to people of fine character.

William H. Strode
Claude L. Brock
Co-Publishers

A one-bottom walking plow with White Rock flock feasting on worms. 1930

A McCormick-Deering tractor and combine. 1926

CONTENTS

J. C. Allen poses with Press Graflex camera in front of his Mitchell touring car. 1919

INTRODUCTION

As time passes, we recall the memories of people, places and events that mean a lot to us. Photos help preserve those precious memories of people and the progress they have made.

"Farming Comes Of Age" preserves the best rural photographs taken in the early 20th Century. Photographs in this book were selected from thousands in the archives of J.C. Allen & Son at West Lafayette, Indiana.

The firm of J.C. Allen & Son has specialized in quality rural photography throughout Midwestern America for over 80 years. J. C. Allen, the founder, began his photo services at a time when agriculture was undergoing many advances. The back-breaking drudgery of farming was succumbing to a more mechanized era. Machines were replacing hand tools, but chores still often required hard work and long hours. The changing times make this collection of photographs quite vivid and penetrating.

"Farming Comes Of Age" contains photographs dating from 1912 to 1942. We selected those that not only represented many changes in agriculture but also illustrated the character and vitality of the times.

The son of a Civil War family, Allen saw the atmosphere of rural America as a treasure. He soon learned how to capture that treasure with the camera. His work is represented in the earliest photos. Son Chester has carried on the photographic tradition set by his father for more than 65 years. Chester's son, John, followed in his father's footsteps and has been a photographer and partner since 1970.

The reliable character of America's rural people has been captured with the camera lenses of the talented Allen family. They have traveled in every nook and cranny throughout the Midwest to record the progress and pulse of modern agriculture as it has developed and unfolded in the 20th Century.

We feel this sampling of more than 200 of the finest rural photographs from an earlier part of this century preserves a bit of important American history.

Thomas Budd, Publisher
Farm Progress Companies

Mary Allen, wife of J. C., gets a lesson in patience when making a photograph of her five-year-old son, Chester, and ducklings in the tub. 1912

PREFACE

The seed for the firm of J.C. Allen & Son was planted in 1904. That was the year my father, J. (John) C. Allen, gave his bride, Mary, a Kodak camera so she could take pictures of their honeymoon trip to the World's Fair in St. Louis. My Mother became very proficient at taking pictures, and Dad always said that she taught him photography.

My Dad started with the Purdue University Department of Animal Husbandry in 1913. He began taking photos with a Graflex camera that was available. The editor of a farm magazine noticed a photograph of a pig he had taken and offered him $2 to use it on his cover. That sale inspired him to take more photos.

J.C. Allen soon had the reputation of being the best livestock photographer around. By 1917, Ohio State University offered him the position of agricultural photographer. The family was packing to move to Ohio when the dean of agriculture at Purdue offered him an office and the opportunity to take all its agricultural photos for a small retainer fee. The rest of the time could be spent taking his own photos. So Dad announced we would not be going to Ohio after all.

When I was growing up, I traveled with my Dad during the summers. I'd carry the equipment, help herd the animals and wave coats to get them to look alert.

I graduated from Purdue in 1929 at the start of the Great Depression. Jobs were few and far between so I started working in the business. I was more

John C. Allen, founder of
J.C. Allen & Son

Mr. and Mrs. Chester P. Allen

John O. Allen, Secretary-Treasurer of J. C. Allen & Son

interested in writing than using a camera at first. But after selling the very first photo I had taken for a farm magazine cover, I was "off and running."

I've never regretted my decision to be the "son" in J.C. Allen & Son Rural Life Photo Service. Despite the Depression, the 1930s were years of growth in our services. Tractors were rapidly replacing horses for power, and tractor companies wanted photos of their new models. We also took a lot of photos for truck and tire companies. Every town of any size had a chick hatchery in those days. There was a great demand for poultry photos to use in advertising.

Edith, my wife of 64 years, accompanied me on most of my journeys, and she helped with many projects through the years. My son, John O., finished his Navy service in 1962, then went to Purdue where he graduated. He worked for a local firm for awhile before becoming the third generation to join J.C. Allen & Son. Dad was active in the business until he passed away at age 94 in 1976.

The earlier photos in this collection were those of J.C. Allen. We are proud to have our photographs selected and published for this book, an idea that we had considered from time to time. They truly represent a photographic history of the development of agriculture from 1912 to 1942. We traveled all over the Midwest, from Nebraska to Ohio and the Dakotas to Missouri and Kansas. There were a few times when we took photos in other parts of the U.S.

I hope you enjoy this selection from the J.C. Allen & Son files. For some readers, the photographs should bring back fond memories as they illustrate the progress made on the farm in a very important era. For still others, we hope our photos enlighten and foster a better understanding of how farming was done once upon a time.

Chester Allen
J.C. Allen & Son
West Lafayette, Indiana

J. C. and Mary Allen working in their flower garden. 1948

Barley harvest. 1927

OUR LAND, OUR HERITAGE

"Let us be grateful for a land so fair, As we raise our voices In a solemn prayer."
—From **God Bless America** by Irving Berlin

The land of America is its soul—that vast resource that has made our nation great. Pause a moment and reflect on those things we take for granted.

It is the land which feeds us, clothes us, helps shelter us, returns energy and sustains our lives.

Like a colorful tapestry, the richness of America's farmland stretches all around us with bounties unmatched. No other country in the world has land which boasts such productive capacity. Much of this abundance comes from the heartland, the 12 Midwestern states, often referred to as the "breadbasket" of the nation. They comprise the most important food-producing area in the world.

Here dark green forests touch lush meadows, gently rolling hills meet flat, rich prairies and meandering streams turn to rushing rivers. The region is usually blessed with favorable temperatures and ample rainfall. Crops are grown and animals thrive.

Of the 100 million acres in the United States rated excellent for growing crops, 75 percent is found in the Midwest. For example, it produces nearly half of the world's corn.

The farmer has readily adapted new science and technology to harness increasing productivity from the land. To the farmer, land has always been another word for soil, and those which cover much of the Midwest are deep and fertile.

In the early 1900s the typical Midwestern farm family literally lived off the land. They kept small flocks of chickens, had orchards and planted gardens. Hogs and cattle were slaughtered at home. A typical farmer produced enough to feed about five people.

Men, women and children toiled together on the land as a family unit. Shocks of drying grain dotted the terrain. Horses pulled heaping racks of shocks to grist mills and threshing machines. Ear corn thumped against bangboards as hand-huskers methodically snapped and pitched like repeating rifles.

It was also during this time that the sound of machines began to echo across the fields, changing the countryside forever. From 1912 to 1942, the true productivity of the land was born. Tractor power and new machines turned Midwestern prairies and plains into bountiful visions of waving grains, tasseled corn and thick stands of lush forage. The image of the farmer was molded into history as a self-sufficient, independent tower of strength during this period.

It was an era of land stewardship filled with nostalgic memories. The J.C. Allen & Son photographs are a reminder of that priceless heritage during a time of great progress on the land. Americans, give thanks that this land is yours.

Monte Sesker, Editor, *Wallaces Farmer*

Summer farm scene. 1927

Cradling wheat during harvest was not an easy task. 1914

Farm couple cradling and hand-tying wheat bundles. 1914

A mother and son shock wheat, a common chore. 1914

Mule power being used for sorghum molasses production. 1926

Grinding sorghum and boiling it down to syrup. 1918

Pitchforks being used to load alfalfa hay on the wagon. 1913

Facing page: Wheat ready for harvest. Circa, 1940

25

Corn planting scene. Circa, 1940s

Farm scene with rail fence. 1933

27

A horse powered feed grinder. 1924

Gathering maple sap to make syrup. 1930

Hand-husking corn. 1939

Ear corn in a wooden crib. 1937

Facing page: Fall farm scene. 1916

31

Red clover field in full bloom. 1932

Cutting and shocking corn. 1942

Storing ear corn in temporary cribs. Circa 1940s

WHEN HORSES WERE KING

"The hoss he is a splendid beast; He is man's friend as heaven destined, and, search the world from west to east, no honester you'll ever find." —From **The Hoss** by James Whitcomb Riley

Horses were an essential part of farm life in the early 1900s. They hauled the corn, milk and hogs to market and supplies from town back to the farm. They transported farmers and their families to neighborhood gatherings and church. And they provided the power to plow, plant and harvest crops.

Farming with horses has made great advances through the years. These advances were driven by the import of heavy draft horse breeds from Europe and improvements in farm implements. Implements included the steel moldboard plow, mowers, rakes, disks, harrows, planters, cultivators and binders.

Powerful horses were needed to pull this machinery. The Percherons from France; Belgians from Belgium; Clydesdales from Scotland; the Shires; and Suffolks from England could do it.

The Percheron was an early favorite. Percheron stallions weighed a ton and could be bred to lighter weight mares to produce horses big and powerful enough for draft work. Thousands of these black and gray Percherons were imported to America.

In the 1920s and 1930s, Belgian horses gained in favor among farmers and surpassed the Percheron in popularity. Belgians were more muscular and short legged — good attributes for working in the field. They also had the reputation for being the gentlest of the draft horse breeds.

Farmers turned increasingly to cars and trucks for their transportation and hauling needs in the 1920s. But while cars were taking over, farm tractors were still large and clumsy.

It wasn't until the development of row-crop tractors in the 1930s that large numbers of farmers began giving up their draft horses for tractors.

Farmers developed a much different relationship with their tractors than they had with their horses. A farmer's horses were almost a part of his family. Horses had names and personalities. Man and horse spent long hours together in the fields. During corn picking, they worked together through the field with the team being directed by simple shouts of "giddyap" and "whoa"or "gee" and "haw".

The conversion from horse to tractor started a new era of farming and closed out the period in which horses were king.

Paul Queck, Editor, *Indiana Prairie Farmer*

Facing page: Corn planting time. 1938

Plowing with three-horse team in front of farmstead. 1932

Scouring the plow before spring work began. 1932

Horses with their shoulders to the plow. 1933

Controlling weeds and chinch bugs with a wooden platform. 1921

Mulching with a log to help control movement of chinch bugs. 1921

Boy drags mower wheel to conserve soil moisture. 1916

Facing page: A father and son plant corn with a one-row planter. 1923

Horse-pulled, two-row planters. 1935

Preparing seedbed and planting corn. 1928

Pretty lass feeding a Percheron colt. 1938

Spreading limestone. 1929

An endgate seeder spreads fertilizer on wheat. 1915

Farmer disks and harrows in one trip. 1921

Rotary hoeing with team of horses. 1934

This four-row corn planter planted 40 acres in one day. 1929

Facing page: Preparing seedbed and drilling oats. 1932

Rotary hoeing with a four-horse hitch. 1930

47

Bareback riding brought a smile to this farm boy. 1930

A boy and his horse become tricksters. 1936

Lending a helping hand. 1932

Rotary hoeing in soybeans. 1934

Horses pulling cultivator in a soybean field. 1923

Facing page: Four sets of cultivators in a check-row field. 1933

51

Green soybeans being cut for hay, followed by a wheat drill. 1914

Drilling wheat between the corn shocks. 1932

Two Deering binders harvesting barley. 1918

A horse drawn corn picker handles the harvest. 1917

Facing page: A binder cutting soybeans, followed by a wheat drill. 1929

*Ten-year-old boy looks at his Dad's **Prairie Farmer**. 1917*

Bobsled provides a winter ride to the mail box. 1936

Mules were used to power the grain elevator. 1915

A farmer husks corn by hand from shocks in the field. 1922

A Percheron team hauls ear corn to the crib. 1938

Pitchforks used to load loose hay. 1934

Loading clover hay. 1929

A farmer hauls milk with his horse and buggy. 1915

Horse and buggy days. Circa, 1920s

A Deering corn picker is pulled by a team of five horses. 1918

Steam engine powers a corn sheller. 1920

A team of horses pulls a Heider tractor from a muddy field. 1921

Preparing for spring seeding. Circa 1930s

Driving the hogs to market. 1913

LIVESTOCK WAS EVERYBODY'S BUSINESS

"I'm going to fetch the little calf That's standing by the mother. It's so young It totters when she licks it with her tongue. I sha'n't be gone long. You come too." —From **The Pasture** by Robert Frost

The era of pioneer farming drew to a close in the early 20th Century. Farmers recognized they could no longer mine the soil by growing crops over and over on the same ground, so many turned to livestock to build a more prosperous agriculture.

Most farmers already raised a few hogs, chickens and dairy cattle to be self-sufficient. But as the 1900s began, farmers started to become more specialized. They began to concentrate on a few crops or a particular kind of livestock for which their land, location or market was well suited. Since little fertilizer was used, advent of the spreader for manure increased use of this valuable soil builder.

Most breeds of livestock grown in the U.S. originated in Europe, although some swine breeds, like the Chester White, are native to America. Farmers also developed a few new ones, like the Duroc and Poland China hog.

Dairying had become a favored occupation in the Lake States where the climate and soil were best suited for forage production. Milk cow numbers in the U.S. grew to 26 to 27 million head in the early 1940s.

Crossbreeding programs to improve rate of gain for beef cattle were also developing. Cattle were beginning to be brought from ranges to feedlots to be grain fed for a more desirable finish. Beef cattle numbers grew steadily as the population increased, and beef was the most popular meat on dinner tables.

Hogs, however, became entrenched as the primary livestock in the Corn Belt. Hogs were called "the mortgage lifters" because of the fast turnover in production and the steady income they could provide. However, market prices didn't always make hogs profitable to raise. The U.S. hog population has risen and fallen with market prices. Hogs were raised for both home use and market on half of the nation's 6.4 million farms in 1919.

More sheep than milk cows and almost as many sheep as hogs could be found on farms in the early 1900s. Wool was the sheep's most important product then, providing farmers with a source of income. A steady decline in wool prices after World War I, was offset by increased value of lamb as meat.

During World War I, egg production was touted as one of the most profitable ventures a farmer could undertake. However, most farmers continued to raise poultry only to meet their own meat and egg needs and make small scale sales until World War II.

Al Morrow, Editor, *Wisconsin Agriculturist*

Two boys bringing in the cows from pasture for milking. 1913

Holstein herd heads for pasture. Circa, 1940s

Feeding Angus steers. 1940

Steers finished on pasture. 1942

Hereford cows and calves on pasture. 1935

Facing page: Dairy herd ready to be milked. Circa, 1940s

73

A happy girl milks her Guernsey cow. 1923

Both the farmer and calf get milk. 1929

A Jersey cow cooperates to provide a Hampshire pig's dinner. 1926

Feeding ear corn to finishing cattle and hogs. 1929

A handsome boy shows off his Guernsey calf. 1931

A dairyman and his dog check the Brown Swiss herd. 1931

Hampshire sows and pigs on typical pasture. Circa, 1940s

Feeding time. 1935

Shoveling ear corn to hogs. 1929

"Sloppin the pigs", as it was called. 1942

Hand powered clippers required two people to shear, an advancement over shearing completely by hand. 1916

Shearing sheep with electric shears. Circa 1940s

Facing page: A farmer and his Collie move the flock. 1915

White Rock laying flock, a common sight. 1940

Placing baby chicks under the brooder. 1939

Feeding White Leghorn hens. Circa, 1940s

Feeding Barred Rock chicks. 1938

Gathering eggs from a White Leghorn flock. 1942

The farm garden was often a big project in itself. 1932

RURAL LIFE: CORNERSTONE OF AMERICA

"Sundays at the farm had a special glow and excitement which nothing else ever surpassed. Always, it seemed, there was something new. Sometimes it was a calf or a litter of puppies, sometimes a rathunt with the big sheep dogs among the standing shocks of corn, sometimes it was maple sugar making, and sometimes a whole troupe of new cousins appeared suddenly from the West on a visit."
— From **The Farm** by Louis Bromfield

There has always been a fascinating oneness about farming in America. The task of farming and farm living are so intertwined that it is impossible to see where one begins and the other ends. On a farm, jobs and home and family round into a full circle of life, unduplicated in other parts of American society.

As the 20th Century began, agriculture was still a primitive culture. It had spread westward over new land, but change came slowly. Farm living remained full of back-breaking labor, hardship, and few frills. Yet, for most it was not an unhappy life. A revolution of machines was incubating that would replace horses with horsepower, multiplying output while making farm tasks easier.

Farm homes were undergoing transformation as well. Settlers moved from primitive houses into more substantial and permanent dwellings.

Much of what America nostalgically immortalizes as ideal living had its roots on early farms. Through the years, traditions of early settlers blended into a homespun mix of values and customs that flourished and became our American heritage.

The drudgery of home care began to ease with modernization of the farm. Washing, ironing and cooking could be done with less time and back-breaking labor. Daily life improved with automobiles and graded roads, bringing markets closer to farmers and rural mail delivery. When electricity came to the farm, it helped bring agriculture closer to the mainstream of American society.

Yet, then as now, farming has been a family culture that sought and found its own joys of living. Farmers, proud of their independence and self reliance, developed farming as a way of life that provided happy times and success just as it provided pain and hardship and despair.

The more things changed in farming in the early half of the 20th Century, the more they stayed the same. Fields had to be tilled. Livestock required care. Meals needed to be cooked. Children went to school. Family values remained important.

Farm living forever demands a constancy of purpose, a steadfastness of mission. It requires a heritage of family and friends and neighbors, guided by the cadence of the seasons and the rhythm of generations. Imitating the cycle of life itself, farming repeats variations of its own theme. . . day-to-day, season-to-season. Farming provides a wholesome, unrelenting pattern in society, counting both good years and disappointing ones like rings on a tree.

Robert L. Bishop, Executive Editor, *Nebraska Farmer*

A community garden club whose members each had a one-eighth acre plot. 1931

Planting the farm garden. 1940

It was noon, but the threshing crew's meal was always called dinner. 1918

Potato harvest. 1934

Digging potatoes was a family project. 1932

This farm's power included a truck, auto, tractor and mule team. 1924

This horse drawn milk wagon had a capacity for 90 cans. 1916

This farm gate could be opened and closed without leaving the automobile. 1918

A Ford and trailer haul a load of milk. 1915

An automobile pulls the horses for a change! 1919

A family moves all its possessions including cattle. 1932

Headed for town in a four-door Dodge. 1937

Holsteins enhance the farmstead. 1940

Using a Case tractor to grind feed. 1932

Hay making time. 1937

A modern farm kitchen with coal range. 1927

Electric-operated cream separator. 1928

Electricity improved work in the home. 1931

Quilting was an art, as well as a popular pastime. 1931

Checker game, an old-fashioned stove and the country general store provide a social atmosphere. 1932

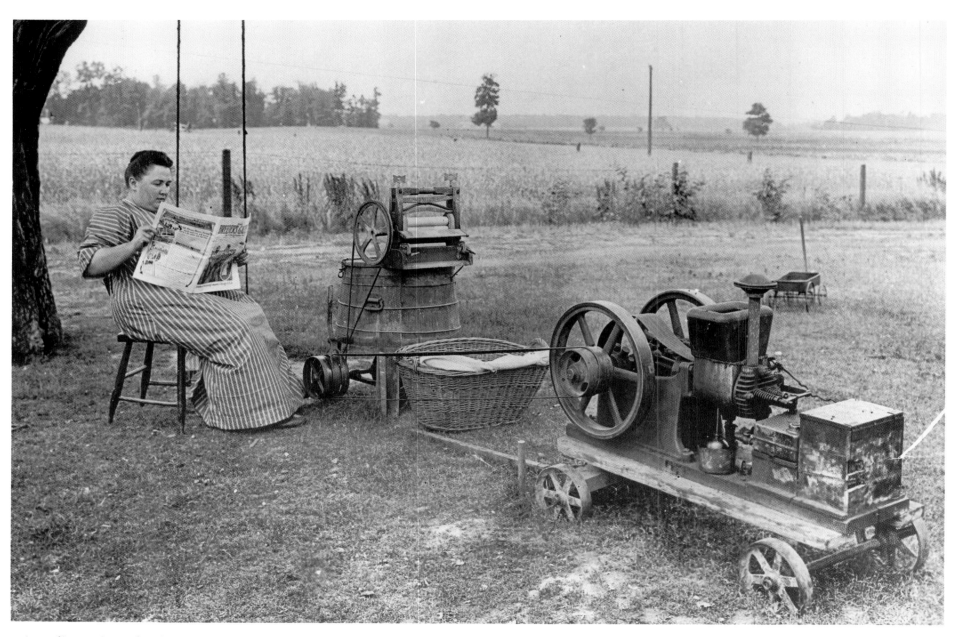

A gasoline engine makes the washing chore easier. 1914

Wash day the old-fashioned way. 1929

A new wringer washer was the best of all. 1926

The huckster made both sales and purchases with farm families. 1928

The country general store was a popular place for shopping. 1926

The consolidated school gradually replaced the one-room school. 1924

The "bibliobus" or traveling library served farms and schools. 1929

A school bus stop. 1930

Horses awaiting their masters' calls. Circa 1920s

The truck parking area at the stock yards. 1929

Traffic on Saturday, the farmer's shopping day. 1931

The whole family chipped-in to make apple cider. 1931

An orchard keeper packs apples into a barrel during harvest. 1915

Making apple butter was a community project. 1925

113

A kerosene lamp aids reading and studying. Circa, 1930s

A Coleman light and iron make domestic work easier. 1926

Electricity brought modern lighting to the farm house. 1935

A farm couple listens to their first radio. 1924

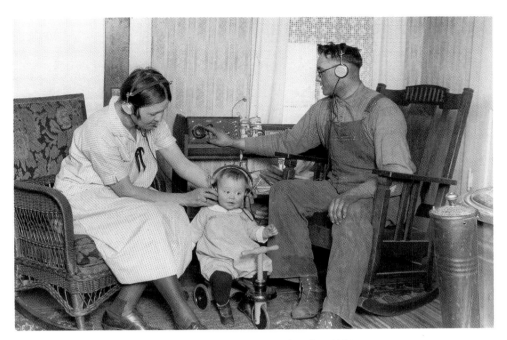

The early radio became a gathering point for the family. 1925

Father and son tune-in their Atwater Kent radio. 1930

A favorite swimming spot in the country. 1929

Fishing was a favorite pastime for farm boys. 1932

Boys cool off on a hot summer day. 1929

This farmer made his own hay loader which was powered by the tractor. 1931

MECHANIZATION OPENS A NEW ERA

"Snub nose, the guts of twenty mules are in your cylinder and transmission. The rear axles hold the kick of twenty Missouri jackasses. It is in the records of the patent office and the ads there is twenty horse power pull here." —From the **New Farm Tractor** by Carl Sandburg

"It was the worst tractor we ever owned." Those were my Dad's less-than-fond memories of the 1917 La Crosse Happy Farmer which also was the first tractor on our family farm. After a few years of constant breakdowns, the Happy Farmer was relegated to the junk pile. The flywheel still serves as a shop anvil stand.

That was the unhappy experience with one of the hundreds of little known tractor names that burst on the rural scene as the early years of the 20th Century soon made way for more reliable equipment. Our family, like thousands of others across the nation, began building loyalties to such great names as Case, International Harvester, Oliver, John Deere and Ford, to name a few.

It is ironic that brand names of farm machinery manufacturers have come mostly through their tractors. Many such manufacturers began operations building something else. J.I. Case was a threshing machine manufacturer. John Deere was a plow maker at first. Henry Ford was an automobile builder and International Harvester could trace its roots to Cyrus McCormick, inventor of the reaper.

It was the machinery pulled or carried by the tractor that really changed the face of agriculture. Without these implements, the tractor was nearly useless. While tractors were built and designed by corporate industries, the machinery more often was designed of necessity by farmers and forged together in farm shops or by local blacksmiths.

It is accepted that tractors and farm implements helped win wars as much as tanks and guns. World War I, with its demand for food, brought good farm prices that helped spawn the early mechanization of farming.

By 1920, there were 229,000 tractors on America's farms. That number doubled in five years, and doubled again by 1930. By 1945, there were over 2 million tractors working on American soil.

Along with improved tractor design and maneuverability came better field tools, from plows to balers in the 1920s and 30s. It was a period of many changes—all aimed to make farming easier.

Larry Harper, Editor, *Missouri Ruralist*

Plowing with an early model tractor. 1918

An Allis-Chalmers with cultipacker and harrow. 1932

Allis-Chalmers, 3 bottom plow and harrow. 1932

Case Model L plowing stalk ground. 1938

Avery tractor pulls a disk. 1918

A Steel-wheeled Huber Model CL plowing in sod. 1936

Minneapolis Moline Model KTA pulling three-bottom plow. 1935

Case Model CC and mounted planter used to plant milo. 1932

Plowing with a John Deere Model B. 1935

Facing page: A farmer plows under clover sod. 1916

Four-row corn planter powered by spike wheel Case. 1932

The Titan pulls a three-bottom Oliver plow. 1918

Steel-wheeled Allis-Chalmers plowing. 1929

A Case tractor pulls a disk as the farmer prepares to sow seed. 1917

Cultivating corn with an early Moline. 1918

This farmer built his own tractor-cultivator. 1923

A homemade cultivator constructed from parts of an old tractor. 1931

An Avery disks corn stalks. 1918

An Avery tractor is used to prepare for wheat seeding. 1917

Homemade cultivator does six rows. 1931

A three-wheeled Allis Chalmers at rest in the field. 1923

Seeding oats with an Avery motor cultivator. 1917

133

Spraying apple trees using a Case tractor. 1933

Spraying the orchard with a Caterpillar Model 22. 1937

Potato digger pulled by a Cletrac. 1940

This farmer designed a soybean harvester that shelled beans. 1922

An IHC tractor and Deering corn picker are used by a farmer as his wife drives the mule team and grain wagon. 1917

Corn harvest in full swing with Fordson and John Deere picker. 1928

Cutting corn for silage using binder pulled by a Wallace tractor. 1916

The Farmall with mounted corn picker pulls the wagon for a clean sweep. 1931

A Moline binder handles the wheat harvest. 1916

Harvesting wheat with a John Deere tractor and McCormick-Deering combine. 1929

Cutting wheat with Fordson tractor. 1925

A crawler tractor pulls three binders at wheat harvest. 1920

Combining soybeans with a Caterpillar and Holt harvester. 1928

A Model T Ford provides belt power for corn shelling. 1923

Horses bring wheat straw to stationary baler. 1933

Baling clover with stationary baler powered by a Hart Parr tractor. 1929

Steam power was used to hull clover seed. 1913

An early, portable hay baler with loader. 1929

Making alfalfa hay with Case tractor and Case pick-up baler. 1932

Cultivating corn with Farmall F-12. 1933

Cultivating corn with mounted cultivator on rubber-tired Farmall tractor. 1933

John Deere Model A tractor equipped with Firestone tires and plow. 1936

Oliver Model 70 Row Crop preparing the seedbed. 1938

Cultivating corn with an Allis Chalmers WC. 1934

Minneapolis Moline Model U with two-row MM Huskor picker. 1942

Plowing with the Silver King. 1936

Plowing with a Case Model R. 1935

Farmall Model F-20 at work. 1936

Ford tractor disking ground. 1941

Allis Chalmers Model U with Goodyear tires plowing in sod. 1937

Disking with an Allis Chalmers W. 1934

This registered Hereford cattle sale drew a big crowd and featured a band. 1914

EVENTS BROUGHT TOGETHERNESS

"The day was hot, but it was dry heat and in the shade the perspiration had little opportunity to collect.
A slow, steady breeze blew across the State Fair grounds, bearing odors of popcorn, cattle, oranges,
drying grass, and humidity. Curiously enough, the blend was not unpleasant." — From **State Fair** by Phil Stong

It was a simpler life in the earlier part of the 20th Century. Yet, it was a fast-moving time too, similar to our pace today in many ways. The automobile, the radio, the telephone and electricity entered rural life from 1912 to 1942. All these removed farm people from isolation and made communication easier than could have been possibly thought by an earlier generation.

Activities for farm families often centered around the church and school. Ice cream socials, fish fries and cake walks not only raised money, but brought people together when they had fewer distractions.

If you were lucky, the traveling circus came to your county seat. The event of the year, however, was the county fair. Young and old alike looked forward to renewing acquaintances and catching up on all the local happenings. They competed for prizes before the judges, and pennies saved all year went for carnival games, a ride on the ferris wheel and cotton candy.

The state fair usually ended the fair season. A visit to the state fair with all its color, sounds, and bustle was the ultimate treat—a trip that left memories long after others faded. The state fair was the showcase for the best of livestock, horticulture and the culinary arts. It took a whole day to take in everything and perhaps longer if you watched the harness races from the grandstand.

There were other events for farm people. Many land grant universities held farmer's week programs with emphasis on new farming techniques. County agents sponsored farm tours. Breed associations had annual picnics, usually on a farm. There were judging contests and trips to the stock yards. In the Midwest, corn husking contests grew in popularity through the 1920s and 1930s. There were county, then state, and finally national champion corn huskers.

The Depression years were tough for farmers. However, they already knew hard times as the boom of the 1920s didn't bring high prices for grain or livestock. Still, they managed to maintain some social life after the crash of 1929.

Farm families often stayed home for rest and recreation in that era, so even an all-day trip to a state park or the lake was something they looked forward to every year. Social activities of farm families might seem meager by today's measure, but events of the era fostered new relationships, fun, and wholesome experiences.

Thomas Budd

A horse pulling contest always drew a crowd. 1928

Judging at a colt show. 1928

Few events were as popular as the state fair as this crowd indicates. 1914

The finish of a state fair harness race brought the grandstand crowd to its feet. 1938

Elaborate displays of fruits, vegetables and grain crops were state fair attractions. 1928

The National Corn Husking Contest at Newtown, Indiana. 1935

No state fair is complete without a Midway. 1935

Lines usually formed at the ferris wheel, the traditional ride at the state fair. 1937

A college demonstration draws a state fair crowd. 1936

State fair activities were an early part of farming's social structure. 1914

APR 1 3 2017

DAUPHIN COUNTY LIBRARY SYSTEM
HARRISBURG, PENNSYLVANIA